THE MOON AND THE MIRROR

THE CAST

The Narrator

Sing Lee

Pitti Sing

Traders One, Two, and Three

NARRATOR: Look – there is a full moon
rising brightly in the sky.
Sing Lee is saying good-bye
to his wife. He has found work
a long way from home, and he
is not sure when he will return.

SING LEE: Good-bye, Pitti Sing.
I hope I have not forgotten anything.
You know what I am like!

PITTI SING: *(laughing)*
Yes, dear husband, you are forgetful.
But we *have* packed everything.

SING LEE: When I return, I shall bring you a gift. Tell me what you would like.

PITTI SING: *(looking at some broken pieces of mirror)* Today I broke my mirror. It is hard for me to do my hair without it. Would you buy me a new one?

SING LEE: Yes, with pleasure!

PITTI SING: To remind yourself, just look at the moon. It is round and bright – just like a mirror. You shall be bringing me a gift that is just like the moon!

NARRATOR: Sing Lee was away for two whole weeks. Then, as a thin, new moon was rising in the sky, he set off home to visit his wife.

SING LEE: Now, I must remember the gift that Pitti Sing wanted. *(He tries to remember.)* Ah – I know what she said: a gift just like the moon! And she wanted to do her hair.

NARRATOR: Sing Lee did not remember that there had been a *full* moon when he left home.

SING LEE: *(He looks up.)* The moon is thin and curved. I will buy a gift that looks like that!

NARRATOR: The next morning,
Sing Lee stopped at a market.

SING LEE: *(looking around)*
All these things are good –
but I need something like the moon.

TRADER ONE: My finest cloth
is as white as the moon!

TRADER TWO: My spoons
are as bright as the moon!

SING LEE: No, what I need is . . .

TRADER THREE: I think I have
what you need. *(He shows Sing Lee
a comb.)*

SING LEE: A comb! Yes!
My wife will be so pleased.

(He pays for the comb and takes it.)

NARRATOR: That evening,
   Sing Lee arrived home.

PITTI SING: Welcome, dear husband!
   You are back at last!

SING LEE: Yes, and here is your gift.
   (He gives her the comb.)
   I looked at the moon last night
   to remember what to buy.

PITTI SING: But I didn't ask for
   a comb. I asked for a mirror!
   Still, the comb is beautiful,
   and I thank you.

SING LEE: Next time, Pitti Sing,
   I will try to remember.

NARRATOR: The next day,
Sing Lee went back to work.
This time, one week passed.
Then, as a half moon was rising
in the sky, he set off again for home.

SING LEE: Now, I shall buy Pitti Sing
her gift – a gift just like the moon.
(He looks up and smiles.)
And look, this time there is no
new moon to trick me!

NARRATOR: The next morning,
Sing Lee stopped once more
at the market.

SING LEE: *(looking around)*
All these things are good –
but I need something like the moon
that I saw last night.

TRADER ONE: My finest cloth
is as white as the moon!

TRADER TWO: My spoons
are as bright as the moon!

SING LEE: No, what I need is . . .

TRADER THREE: I think I have
what you need. *(He shows Sing Lee
a silver hair clasp, shaped
like a half moon.)*

NARRATOR: That evening,
Sing Lee arrived home.

PITTI SING: Welcome, dear husband!
You are back again!

SING LEE: Yes, and here is your gift!
(He gives her the hair clasp.)
I looked at the moon very carefully
to remember what to buy.

PITTI SING: Now I have a new comb
and a fine silver hair clasp.
But the moon has tricked you again.
And I still do not have a mirror
so that I can *see* my hair!

SING LEE: Next time, Pitti Sing,
I will try even harder to remember.

NARRATOR: And so Sing Lee,
for the third time, went off to work.
One week passed. Then, one rainy
night, he set off home.

SING LEE: This time, I am sure
that I can remember the right gift.
I shall look at the moon
to remind me, and this time
I will not let it trick me!
(He looks up.)

NARRATOR: But the moon
was covered by clouds!

SING LEE: What will I do?
I do not want to take Pitti Sing
the wrong thing again!
*(He sits down and puts his head
in his hands.)*

SING LEE: *(looking at a pool of water)*
What is this? What a beautiful sight!
The pool is just like a mirror –
and I can see the moon in it,
bright and round! Now I remember
what Pitti Sing wanted!

21

SING LEE: *(At the market)*
I don't want any cloth.
I don't want any spoons.
I want a mirror – as round
and bright as the full moon.

TRADER THREE: Why didn't you
say so before? *(He brings out a mirror.)*

SING LEE: That is exactly what I want!
(He pays for the mirror and takes it.)

NARRATOR: Sing Lee rushed home
as quickly as he could.

SING LEE: Pitti Sing! Pitti Sing!
Here is your gift!

PITTI SING: You remembered!
And what a beautiful mirror!
I asked for *one* gift that was
like the moon. Now I have three.
I will never forget how kind you are.

SING LEE: And *I* will never forget
how the moon changes!